CHRISTMAS DECORATIONS

CHRISTMAS DECORATIONS

OVER 35 GLORIOUS PROJECTS

JANE NEWDICK
PHOTOGRAPHY PIA TRYDE

CRESCENT BOOKS
NEW YORK • AVENEL, NEW JERSEY

Text copyright © Jane Newdick 1993
Photography copyright © Ebury Press 1993
(except photographs on pages 8–9, 13 and 37, © Country Living Magazine)

Jane Newdick has asserted her right to be identified as the author of this work.

First published in the UK in 1993 by Ebury Press
This 1994 edition published by
Crescent Books, distributed by
Outlet Book Company, Inc.,
a Random House Company
40 Engelhard Avenue
Avenel, New Jersey 07001

Random House
New York · Toronto · London · Sydney · Auckland

Art Director: GEORGINA RHODES
Editor: JOANNA COPESTICK

ISBN 0-517-10247-1

Typeset by Textype Typesetters, Cambridge
Printed and bound in Portugal by Printer Portuguesa

CONTENTS

❧

INTRODUCTION

Whether it is simple garlands of greenery used at the earliest mid-winter festivities or our sophisticated trees smothered with fripperies, few of us have ever been able to resist decorating the home for Christmas. Much of the pleasure comes from rediscovering the decorations which were packed away the previous year or finding a special new decoration to add to the family collection. This part of the fun is almost more exciting than seeing the house finished and decorated, especially if you have made the decorations yourself. *Christmas Decorations* has lots of ideas to inspire you, some completely new and some based on traditional themes. The projects are separated into two chapters: *Fruits & Flowers, Berries & Boughs* contains ideas for using natural materials, many of which you can find around you in the countryside; *Papers & Paints, Cottons & Candles* concentrates on all the wonderful things you can do with a huge variety of fabrics, papers, paints and other materials. From the simplest wreath to more elaborate looking sewing projects, none of the ideas takes a long time to create and some notes on equipment on pages 94–95 explain the minimal things you need. Happy Christmas decorating.

Jane Newdick

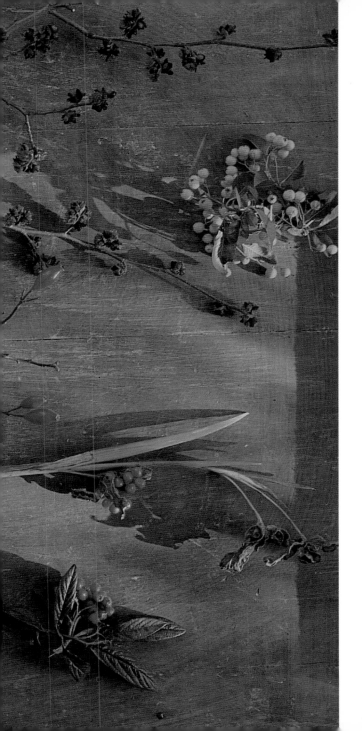

*Fruits &
flowers,
berries &
boughs*

❧

CARVED CITRUS FRUITS

These sculpted fruits look beautiful arranged on a tall-stemmed cake stand or simply placed in a large shallow bowl. You could add shiny green bay leaves, sprigs of rosemary or myrtle or ivy leaves under or in-between the citrus fruits as a variation on the basic idea. Limes and lemons are the easiest fruits to work on as are small and firm oranges but satsumas are too soft to carve easily and clementines are very thin skinned and therefore difficult to use. Save the discarded peel for other decorations or dry them to use as food flavourings or as ingredients for pot pourris. If the fruits are sound and unwaxed or untreated, they will dry naturally and can be displayed for many months.

MATERIALS

A mixture of lemons, oranges, limes etc. ❧ *a peel cutter (known as a canelle knife)*

1. The fruits should be as firm and as fresh as possible and preferably untreated. If not, scrub and clean the skin.

2. A canelle knife is a small knife with a blade which has a sharpened notch just under 6mm (¼in) wide which cuts a groove into the skin. Use this to trace patterns over the fruit.

3. Apply horizontal parallel lines to some fruits and rows of vertical lines to others. Or try making scroll-like patterns or concentric circles all over the fruits. Once you gain confidence you can cut all kinds of patterns, so have fun experimenting.

HEART WREATH

Berry decorations can be hung outside on a door or a tree, where they will not only look good but will also keep birds supplied with the food they need to take them through the winter. This very quick yet effective wreath uses a simple metal coathanger as the frame.

MATERIALS

Metal coathanger ❧ *about 10 medium-length supple pine twigs, with cones attached* ❧ *small green leaves* ❧ *small bunches of berries (any brightly coloured varieties)* ❧ *fine wire* ❧ *wire cutters*

1. Bend the wire coathanger into a heart shape and cut off the hooked end.

2. Wind the twigs around the wire and finish neatly by threading any loose ends in securely. If any wire is still showing, cover it with small leaves.

3. Using the fine wire, attach the small bunches of berries to the wreath at regular intervals.

4. Make a loop of wire at the top of the wreath on which to hang it up.

LICHEN TREE

You could make a pair of miniature trees if you prefer, so as to have a symmetrical decoration. The gold doves were bought from a shop selling cake decorations. Look out for similar objects which would make pretty additions to the lichen branches. Collect lichen from fallen tree branches and store it for later use. It can be used successfully fresh from the bark or dried.

MATERIALS

Terracotta plant pot about 10cm (4in) in diameter ❧ section of silver birch or similar branch about 15cm (6in) long ❧ plaster or Polyfilla ❧ Plasticine or floral putty ❧ moss ❧ Polystyrene ball about 12.5cm (5in) in diameter ❧ glue gun ❧ lichen ❧ plastic doves painted gold ❧ a few shreds of gold metal scouring pad

1. Fill hole in plant pot with Plasticine or putty. Mix up plaster or Polyfilla according to instructions.

2. Stand stem in pot and wedge securely with Plasticine or putty. Pour in plaster or Polyfilla and leave to set, then cover top surface with moss.

3. Push Polystyrene ball onto stem securely. Cover surface of ball with glue then attach tufts of lichen, working over one small area at a time.

4. Add a few strands of metal scouring pad by tucking them in amonst the lichen. Glue a few gold doves onto the lichen.

APPLE & ORANGE GARLANDS

This is one of the simplest ideas in the book and one of the most effective. Choose deep red- or scarlet-skinned apples or alternatively use a bright green variety such as Granny Smith.

MATERIALS

Red-skinned apples (each apple makes approximately six to ten rings, depending on its size) ❧ *salt solution* ❧ *kitchen paper* ❧ *orange peel* ❧ *medium wire*

1. Mix up the salt solution using 50g (2oz) salt to 3.5L (6pts) of water.

2. Slice the apples with a sharp knife into rings about 3mm (⅛in) thick and drop them immediately into the brine. Leave for about 10 minutes or so while you finish cutting the rest of the apples.

3. Pat the apple rings dry with kitchen paper and thread them onto a length of wire, leaving a small space between them as much as possible. Hang the apples up to dry horizontally above a warm cooker or in an airing cupboard. They will take several days to dry to a leathery texture.

4. Meanwhile, thread strips of orange peel onto lengths of wire and hang these to dry in the same way.

5. When everything is ready, rethread the apples, but this time add pieces of orange peel between every 3 or 4 rings. Leave as long garlands to hang or drape or make into wreaths.

TWIG-WRAPPED GILDED GLOBES

These stylish sculptural golden globes are wrapped with lengths of twining wild clematis. Long, tough clematis stems are ideal for the job as they are very strong but flexible. Vine stems are suitable too, or any kind of climbing plant. Gold leaf sheets are expensive but go a long way and though it is possible to get real 24-carat gold leaf, imitation leaf will do just as well. For the best effect, make a group of globes of different sizes.

MATERIALS

Cotton waddding or Polystyrene balls (available from craft and model shops) ❧ *gold leaf sheets* ❧ *Spray-Mount glue* ❧ *lengths of wild clematis stem* ❧ *scalpel blade or sharp knife* ❧ *flat stick or spoon handle*

1. Spray the balls with glue and carefully lift gold leaf in to place. It is easiest to do this in small areas at a time, picking up the sheets from their tissue backing with a scalpel blade or sharp knife. Pat gold leaf into place with a flat stick or spoon handle or use a dry, clean finger. You are not aiming for a perfect finish.

2. When each ball is gilded, begin to wrap a length of clematis around it, twisting and turning it as you go so as to cover the ball in different directions, like winding a ball of wool. As one length is finished, tuck the end under another stem and add more if necessary. Aim to leave the golden globe showing through in several places.

STRINGS OF LEAVES & SPICES

These look good hung on the Christmas tree or strung across a room. The large leaves of eucalyptus are easily obtained by buying a branch or two of fresh eucalyptus from a flower shop and hanging it to dry naturally in a warm place. When it is dry snip off the whole leaves to use.

MATERIALS

Lengths of narrow flat tape or ribbon ❧ *dried eucalyptus leaves* ❧ *dried oak leaves* ❧ *dried berries and chillies* ❧ *cloves* ❧ *cinnamon sticks* ❧ *nuts in their shells* ❧ *kumquats* ❧ *dried apple rings* ❧ *any other decorative fruits, leaves, dried flowers etc* ❧ *glue gun or glue*

Make several strings using slightly different arrangements. Leave a regular space between each item attached to the ribbon. You can make a recurring pattern of decorative bits or mix things randomly along the ribbon.

1. Cut a tiny slot through each dried leaf near an edge. Thread ribbon through the holes then knot in place. You can also glue leaves flat to ribbon. Decorate some leaves with extra details such as berries, chillies or spices.

2. Tie tiny bundles of cinnamon together and tie to ribbon.

3. Glue kumquats and nuts to ribbon. Thread apple rings onto the ribbon and then knot securely.

GILDED OAK LEAF WREATH

This may require a little forward planning if you are to have oak leaves at Christmas. On small oak trees, the brown leaves stay on the branch until the following spring, so they can be gathered whenever you choose. Otherwise, collect good specimens when they are shed in autumn and press them flat between newspaper and weight them. Once gilded they can be used for all kinds of different decorations. The oak-leaf shape is a pretty and unexpected alternative to more traditional Christmas evergreens. To make the best gold paint, use a clear medium and loose bronze powder mixed together.

MATERIALS

Clear paint medium (try clear lacquer or Ormoline metallic paint medium) ❧ *bronze powder in middle gold* ❧ *emerald green metallic powder* ❧ *dried oak leaves* ❧ *wire wreath frame* ❧ *glue gun*

1. Mix a small amount of medium with the gold powder and another batch with the green powder.

2. Using a brush, or a small natural sponge if you find it easier, paint one side of each oak leaf and leave to dry.

3. Using a glue gun, place the leaves around the wire frame, adding a few green ones amongst the gold.

4. For a neat effect keep them all facing one way.

GREEN & WHITE FRESH FLOWERS

It is the greatest treat to have fresh flowers in the house at Christmas, but this will invariably call for a trip to the flower shop to augment the garden offerings which you may have. At least you should already have some evergreen foliage to help out, or perhaps a few early hellebores around which to build an arrangement. A cool bowlful of scented flowers is a welcome visual relief against Christmas decorations made from everything imaginable.

MATERIALS

To fill a small bowl: three stems white lilac ❧ two stems small-flowered white lilies ❧ three stems green hellebores ❧ one bunch white ranunculus ❧ one bunch chincherinchees ❧ four stems white wax flower ❧ viburnum tinus ❧ garden evergreens ❧ green floral foam ❧ white bowl

1. Trim all stems of flowers and shrubs and soak the floral foam until damp right through. Cut and fit the foam into the bowl.

2. Begin by making a framework from the foliage and viburnum tinus, if you are using it, all over the bowl, keeping the whole arrangement quite low and spreading.

3. Put the lilac stems in place, equally spaced through the bowl. Add the hellebores, then the wax flowers.

4. Finally, add the lilies, chincherinchees and ranunculus.

SPICE, BERRY & PETAL BALLS

This simple idea is a starting point for all kinds of decorations. You will find many other things which can be glued to the basic ball shape apart from the spices, berries, and dried flower petals we show here. The finished spheres look lovely piled into a large bowl or stacked in a pyramid shape or they can have strings attached to them and be hung up. A glue gun certainly makes the process very quick and easy, but if you don't have one you can use an all-purpose glue with the same, but slightly slower, results. The ready-made balls are generally white, so if the surface decoration is not tightly packed together the white shows through. If this is a problem, paint the ball first in a dark colour. Some Polystyrene balls melt slightly on contact with the hot glue. It doesn't matter, because the whole surface is eventually covered over.

MATERIALS

Cotton wadding or Polystyrene balls in different sizes (available from craft and model shops) ❧ *dried flower petals such as rose or hydrangea* ❧ *allspice* ❧ *juniper berries* ❧ *peppercorns* ❧ *cloves* ❧ *dried hawthorn berries (available from wine-making shops)* ❧ *glue gun or glue* ❧ *black or brown water-based paint (optional)*

1. Work on a small area of the ball at a time. With a glue gun you have to be quick, so attempt to glue three or four spices, or one petal, at a time.

2. Cloves may need to have some of their stem cut off so that you glue just the berry part to the surface. Continue until the whole ball is covered.

FROSTED FRUITS

This idea is often used to make festive table decorations, sometimes with a view to the fruits being eaten as a dessert. If you choose firm and slightly under-ripe fruit, the whole thing will keep for several days, or at least for the duration of the main Christmas festivities. Choose fruit in a variety of shapes, size and colours. Grapes are the usual choice and always look wonderful, but search out a few more exotic and unusual fruits too. You can even use whole nuts in their shells. Finely, a mixture of fine and coarse sugar for the frosting gives a pleasing glittery and contrasting texture.

MATERIALS

A variety of fruits (green and purple grapes, pears, apples, mangoes, plums, lychees, limes etc.) 🍃 *dried pressed leaves (optional)* 🍃 *caster sugar* 🍃 *granulated sugar* 🍃 *egg white*

1. Gently beat the egg white until foamy.

2. Using a pastry brush, paint the egg white over the fruits and leaves.

3. Sprinkle and dip the fruits and leaves into either caster sugar or granulated sugar, or a mixture of the two.

4. Leave the fruits to dry separately on a wire rack in a warm place.

5. When the sugar and egg white is crisp and dry, pile the fruits into a basket and tuck a few of the leaves in amongst them, if using.

A KISSING BOUGH

This is based on the traditional kissing bough which has been made for mid-winter festivities from the earliest times.

MATERIALS

Three wire coat hangers ❧ fine wire ❧ one red apple ❧ cord or string ❧ lengths of small-leaved ivy ❧ small bunch of mistletoe ❧ pliers ❧ red ribbon

1. Stretch each wire coat hanger from below the hook to make a ring shape. Take one hanger and wire it to the second at top and bottom. Add the third hanger and attach in same way with fine wire, twisting it tightly in place with pliers.

2. Shape and bend the hangers to make a three-dimensional globe with the six vertical wires evenly spaced.

3. Bend the three hooks at the top to face the same way or cut off two hooks with wire cutters, leaving just one. Twine lengths of ivy around the six wires. Attach with fine wire or thread if necessary.

4. Push a skewer through the centre of the apple, remove it and thread a cord through the hole. Tie a knot at the bottom and put a tiny twig or matchstick in the knot to stop the cord pulling through. Hang the apple inside the globe and attach cord to hook. Finish with a bow of red ribbon.

SCENTED POSY

This scented posy is made from a bunch of dried ranunculus and a stem fashioned from cinnamon sticks. You could also use dried roses or indeed any dried flowers that have a solid shape. Add extra scent by dropping essential oil onto the flower petals and replenish it when the fragrance fades.

MATERIALS

6 cinnamon sticks, approximately 14cm (5½in) long ❧ about 40 dried flower heads such as ranunculus, preferably on stems ❧ short stub wires (optional) ❧ fine wire ❧ glue ❧ about 1m (1yd) ribbon ❧ essential oil e.g. cinnamon, rose, or orange

1. If the flowers do not have stems, wire or glue each of the flower heads to stub wires.

2. Bunch the flowers into a posy, keeping them tightly packed, to create a round shape. To hold the posy together, wire the stems tightly just beneath the flowers. Glue the cinnamon sticks, one at a time, onto the posy stem until it is fully enclosed.

3. Tie the ribbon around the cinnamon handle and finish with a fat bow. Trim the ribbon edges neatly.

4. Using a small eye dropper, apply drops of essential oil to the flowers. If the posy is to be hung up, attach a fine wire to the back of the cinnamon handle to create a loop or wrap it around the handle so that it is hidden underneath the ribbon.

FRUIT BASKET

This crown of fruit can adorn a Christmas table, or make a festive nest to be placed on a special friend's or neighbour's doorstep. Use a basket with a closely woven top and collect berries and leaves on the day (or day before) they were needed, so that they look plump and fresh.

MATERIALS

Wicker basket ❧ brightly coloured berries ❧ leaves ❧ fine wire, cut into 10cm (4in) lengths ❧ wire cutters ❧ apples, pears and oranges

1. Arrange the berries in small bunches and twist wire around the stems to secure them.

2. Lay the bunches along the top of the basket at even intervals, then thread the ends of the wire through gaps in the top of the basket and secure them carefully on the inside. Trim off any surplus wire.

3. Weave in some individual leaves between and under the bunches of berries, using them to cover the wire if necessary.

4. Finish by piling high with fresh fruit.

TWIG CHANDELIER

This decoration can be used as a hanging chandelier, or it can sit flat on a surface or be hung up as a wreath. If the candles are lit, never leave the room unattended.

MATERIALS

A wire wreath frame approximately 46cm (18in) in diameter ❧ long lengths of a pliable climber such as clematis or vine ❧ fine wire ❧ small sprigs of eucalyptus (ours were dyed deep maroon) ❧ 10 to 12 clip-on tree candle holders ❧ candles

1. Begin by sorting out some long lengths of climber and removing any side branches or buds from them.

2. Start to twine a length through the wire frame, working round the circle and tucking the ends securely in place. If the stems are not very pliable, you may need to wire them to the frame.

3. Continue until the frame is covered and cannot be seen through the twigs. Clip the candle holders in place. If you intend to hang the chandelier, continue to steps four to five.

4. Knot three lengths of stem to the frame at equidistant points round the circle. Wire these to the frame. Hold up the chandelier and adjust the lengths of the stems so that it hangs evenly and horizontally.

5. Tie the three stems together at the top and wire securely. Finally, wire on a few pieces of eucalyptus to hang down beneath the frame.

HYACINTH BOWL

Hyacinths are among the first winter flowering bulbs and white varieties always look particularly festive. The tall, heavy heads of flowers invariably need support, so the project exploits this need, while looking very pretty in the process. You could use the same idea for any flowering plant which needs a supporting structure. Use a strong twig such as hazel or willow; if you can't pick your own, then a small bought cane or plant support would do.

MATERIALS

Growing hyacinth bulbs to fill a shallow terracotta bowl ❧ *fresh moss* ❧ *several straight twigs* ❧ *a hazelnut in its shell for each twig* ❧ *gold paint* ❧ *gold cord* ❧ *tassel* ❧ *glue gun*

1. Plant up the bulbs if not home grown and cover the soil in the bowl with a layer of fresh moss.

2. Push twigs, all the same length, into the inside edge of the bowl and space them evenly around it.

3. Paint hazelnuts with gold paint or lacquer and, when dry, glue one to the top of each twig, pointed end upwards.

4. Loop gold cord around the twig structure, tying it around each twig and gluing it in place for security. Tie the two ends of the cord neatly together. Finish off by tying a piece of tasseled cord around the bowl.

TALL TREE WITH MARZIPAN PEARS

This elegant tree could be used in place of a traditional Christmas tree.

MATERIALS

Container ❧ *green floral foam* ❧ *small-mesh chicken wire* ❧ *silver birch branch* ❧ *plaster or Polyfilla* ❧ *branches of blue spruce* ❧ *narrow green ribbon* ❧ *marzipan* ❧ *pink food colour* ❧ *cloves* ❧ *fine and medium wire* ❧ *hanging tree decorations*

1. Stand branch centrally in an old container, fill it up with plaster or Polyfilla, then leave to set.

2. Cut damp floral foam pieces and put together to make a rough cube. Wrap this in chicken wire to hold it together. We used two separate pieces to make a cube about 18 x 18 x 18cm (7 x 7 x 7 in).

3. Push the cube down over top of stem in pot and secure with medium wire if necessary. Start to push short branches of spruce into foam to make a roughly triangular shape.

4. Hang small decorations all over tree and tie a little ribbon bow where each one is fixed to the branch.

5. Make small pear shapes out of marzipan. Add a pink blush using food colour. Use a clove stem to make the pear stalk. Push fine wire right through the fruit, just under stalk, and twist together. Use this to hang each pear from the branches.

DRIED FLOWER & LEAF GARLAND

This large-scale garland can be used as a decoration indoors or as an alternative to a wreath on a front door. It is made from warm brown leaves, small pieces of Scots pine, ivy berries and subtly coloured dried roses and is a welcome variation on the usual Christmas garland made entirely from evergreens and berries. It could be dressed up further with clusters of ribbons or bows.

MATERIALS

A wire wreath frame approximately 46cm (18in) in diameter ❧ small bunches of dried oak leaves ❧ stems of deep maroon eucalyptus leaves ❧ pieces of Scots pine ❧ dried roses in several colours ❧ ivy berries ❧ a few small pine cones ❧ glue gun

1. Lie the frame on a large flat surface and begin by covering it with the oak leaves, twisting the stems through the wire. You may need to glue or wire these to secure them, but if the stems are long enough they will hold themselves in place.

2. Add pieces of Scots pine, gluing the stems to other stems or the wire frame. Work round the frame, spacing them evenly.

3. Add stems of eucalyptus so they radiate from the centre of the frame.

4. Now begin to add decorative roses, small clusters of ivy berries or other dried berries. Space these as naturally as possible, so that they appear to be growing out of the leafy background.

RED AMARYLLIS & LEAVES

Brilliant red amaryllis make sumptuous Christmas decorations and need very little embellishment. Handle them gently, as their enormous stems are hollow and therefore quite fragile. They may seem expensive to buy compared to other cut flowers but they have the advantage of lasting for many days in water. Placed in a window recess their bold shape and outline and the velvety texture of their vivid petals can be fully appreciated.

MATERIALS

Stems of red amaryllis ❧ tall clear glass vases ❧ crumpled clear cellophane ❧ fresh laurel leaves or other winter greenery ❧ double-sided tape ❧ gold cord

1. Cut stems anew if they have been out of water long and stand them in the vases ,with water about a third of the way up the sides.

2. Place some crumpled cellophane into the water in the vase, to add sparkle and help support the stems.

3. Attach a strip of double-sided tape around the top outside edge of the vase and press a row of leaves along it, slightly overlapping each one.

4. Wind a length of gold cord around the leaves and tie tightly, leaving short ends. If the cord is inclined to fray, wrap adhesive tape around it before cutting pieces through the middle of the tape.

SILVER TWIG BUNDLE

This silver bundle looks marvellous hanging from a door or gate. The twigs can be fresh or dried, but in either case they should be smooth, with any buds or branches removed. We used dogwood stems from a garden shrub which had a good smooth bark. Experiment to find the best silver spray paint as they vary enormously, some are very dull and hardly metallic, while others look exactly like real silver. For this project you really do have to resort to a spray, as painting the twigs by hand would be out of the question.

MATERIALS

Bundle of twigs, roughly the same thickness and about 46cm (18in) long ❧ *silver spray paint* ❧ *medium wire* ❧ *long lengths of small-leaved ivy* ❧ *silver ribbon*

1. Gather the twigs into a bundle, letting them bend naturally outwards if they wish, leaving the ends fairly uneven. Bind the centre of the twigs tightly together with a length of medium wire.

2. Spray the twigs with silver paint, moving the bundle around to be sure that you cover all surfaces. Leave to dry.

3. Wrap a length or two of fresh ivy around the middle of the bundle and tuck in the loose ends or wire them to the bundle.

4. Attach a long length of silver ribbon through the wire at the centre in order to hang the bundle from a door or gate.

LEAF TABLE DECORATION

This is a very simple way to create a special place-setting for a Christmas meal. You could place the leaf border straight on to a polished wood table where it would look rich and traditional, or on a cloth, either patterned or plain white, to frame your favourite china. All you need is a good source of large leaves, such as these which we used from an ivy, or you could use dried pressed leaves, or the golden oak leaves used for the garland on page 20. Earlier this century, children spent hours sewing leaves together or onto fabric to make Christmas banners and decorations.

MATERIALS

Large, plain ivy leaves ❧ small, variegated ivy leaves ❧ fine wire

1. Sort out the leaves to roughly the same size and snip off any stalks attached to the leaves.

2. Lay one leaf half way over another and push a little loop of fine wire through both leaves from the front. Twist the wire to fasten at the back.

3. Add more leaves, one at a time, in the same way. Each new leaf should cover the wire on the leaf before. When the top edge is the right size, turn a corner and work on a vertical row.

4. Continue round to make a complete frame. Tuck small ivy leaves between the large ones. This should hold them in place without the need for wire.

TALL MOSS TREE & STAR

Fresh green bun moss will dry out slowly and allow the decoration to keep for many months. To fix the stem in the container you could also use plaster (see page 44) if you do not want to use the container again.

MATERIALS

Shallow terracotta container (square or round) ❧ *dried flower foam* ❧ *twigs* ❧ *foam cone* ❧ *fine wire* ❧ *fresh bun moss* ❧ *gold ribbon* ❧ *gold star (we made one from Fimo and painted it gold)*

1. Cut and fit some dried flower foam into the container and cover the top with bun moss.

2. Tie five or six twigs together and wire at top and bottom to make the stem. Push one end securely into the base. Push foam cone onto stem, being careful to keep it centrally in place as you push.

3. Attach fine wire to stem just under cone and start to put pieces of moss on foam, wrapping wire around generously as you go. Two pairs of hands make this job much simpler. Keep adding moss and wrapping wire to hold it in place, covering all the foam. Spray to keep it fresh.

4. Push the star, fixed to a stick or twig, down into the cone from above. Wrap the tree stem with a twist of gold ribbon, tucking the ends in neatly.

5. Scatter a few tiny glass baubles amongst the moss in the pot if you wish.

Papers &
paints,
cottons &
candles

☙

BROCADE TREASURE BAGS

Make these luxurious bags with remnants of extravagant fabric such as damask, brocade, duchesse satin, chiffon or organdy. To tie the finished bags, use glossy cord or gold braid and embellish them with toning ribbon in satin, taffeta or velvet. The basic big shape is made from a single piece of fabric folded in half and sewn up two sides. It is made very tall so that extra fabric is tucked back down inside the bag and hidden when the bag is tied. These instructions are for a narrow rectangular bag.

MATERIALS

Pieces of fabric ❧ ribbon ❧ cord ❧ trimming (optional) ❧ sewing thread

1. Cut a piece of fabric approximately 40 x 8cm (15½ x 3¼in).

2. Fold it in half, right sides together, across the middle.

3. Stitch along the two long edges, making a seam of about 1cm (⅜in). Turn right side out and press.

4. Turn top 6cm (2¼in) of the fabric inwards and press the top edge.

5. Fill the bag with treasure and tie a piece of cord or ribbon tightly around the top to secure.

6. For extra decoration, add tassels to the cord or ribbon or tie on a small tree decoration.

OYSTER-SHELL CANDLES

The candles will burn for about two hours, long enough for a festive meal.

MATERIALS

White candle wax granules ❧ beeswax (use about one quarter beeswax to three quarters wax granules) ❧ wick to fit ❧ double saucepan ❧ deep halves of empty oyster shells ❧ candle putty or Plasticine ❧ wooden sticks or skewers

1. To clean the shells boil in a pan of water for 3 minutes, and dry.

2. Fix a short length of wick to the centre of base of shell using a tiny blob of candle putty or Plasticine. The wick should suit the size of shell, about 5cm (2in) in diameter, and be slightly longer than finally required.

3. Lay stick across top of shell and hang wick over this, centring it as much as possible. Hold wick in place on stick with small piece of Plasticine.

4. Prop shells on flat surface using more Plasticine. Carefully melt wax and beeswax in a double saucepan and when melted pour quickly but gently into waiting shells.

5. When wax has set it may have shrunk so you can top up with a little more melted wax if you wish. When completely cold and set hard, remove stick and trim wick to about 1.5cm (½in).

6. Before lighting candles, make sure they are standing safely and are not likely to topple over. Tuck them in to a bed of crushed ice.

PAPERCHAINS

Paperchains are delightful traditional Christmas decorations. Our version of the idea uses several different types of decorative paper in three colours, with extra details on each loop that include pinked edges and cut-out holes. Any paper is suitable for this treatment, as long as it can be glued or joined with double-sided tape. It should ideally be reversible, as the inside of the chains will show. It is the sort of project which is fun to make in a group, to speed things up. The measurements here make quite small chains which are prettier than large clumsy ones, but you can vary the size according to where you plan to put them. Miniature ropes of chains look lovely on a Christmas tree.

MATERIALS

Several different types of paper in red, green and gold, preferably coloured on both sides ❧ *scissors* ❧ *craft knife* ❧ *metal rule or cutting edge* ❧ *paper glue or double-sided tape* ❧ *pinking shears* ❧ *hole punch*

1. Work on a large, clean, flat surface and cut out lots of basic strips using a craft knife and cutting edge. Our strips were 2x16cm (¾x6⅓in).

2. Cut some strips with pinked edges and some with scalloped edges.

3. Use a hole punch to make regular or random patterns in some of the strips. Try other decorative details.

4. Mixing different designs, glue the chains together, or use double-sided tape, until you have long chains.

PAINTED GLASS

Glass can be decorated with special indelible glass paint which is transparent. It can be slightly difficult to use as the liquid has to be quite thick in order to adhere to the smooth, non-porous surface of glass. The easiest designs to attempt are simple freehand patterns, spots or wavy lines. The range of glass shown here, with its raised edges made up of small spheres, made decorating easy. The paint was applied to the underneath surface of each ball and shone through prettily. Look out for pressed glass with raised designs which can be blocked in with paint, or a single motif which can be painted.

MATERIALS

Glass plates, bowls, tumblers etc. ❧ *glass paint* ❧ *glass paint thinner* ❧ *brushes*

1. Make sure the glass to be painted is absolutely clean and free from grease. Test your chosen paint on a small piece of scrap glass to check colour and consistency.

2. If the paint is very thick, thin it down slightly with glass paint thinner so that it is easy to brush on smoothly. (Gold glass paint will need plenty of stirring to distribute the pigments.)

3. Work on a small area at a time and wipe away any smudges or mistakes quickly with thinners.

4. Leave to dry in a clean place.

SALT DOUGH SHAPES

Sometimes salt dough is coloured or painted after baking, but the pale creamy dough colour is pleasing left as it is. You can egg-glaze it to make it look more like real bread, or bake it blind then varnish or glaze it later. These small garlands are easy to copy and involve rolling and moulding the fruit and flower shapes in your hands.

MATERIALS

For at least 3 small sculptures: 100g (4oz) plain white flour ✿ 100g (4oz) cooking salt ✿ 100ml (4floz) cold water ✿ whole cloves ✿ egg yolk and milk (optional)

1. Put the flour and salt into a large bowl and mix well together. Add the water while stirring the mixture and continue mixing until you have a manageable dough.

2. Put the dough on a floured board and knead it with your hands.

3. Wrap the dough in a plastic bag and leave it to rest for about an hour.

4. Roll out dough and shape it. Join the pieces with a dab of water. Make fruits and round shapes by rolling dough into balls in your hand. Use cloves to make stalks and calyxes on fruits.

5. If you wish to glaze the dough, brush with a mixture of egg yolk and milk before baking in a cool oven, gas mark 2, 150°C (300°F) until it is hard but not over browned (about an hour).

CHRISTMAS TREE SHAPES

Choose simple shapes for these decorations otherwise they will become fiddly to make. Don't expect them to be completely accurate, in fact they look more charming for being a little imperfect. Experiment with different surface decorations such as sequins and braids, or embroidered motifs, beads and pearls.

MATERIALS

Pieces of fabric, preferably silk or a similar soft fabric ❧ *polyester loose filling (wadding)* ❧ *sewing thread* ❧ *decorations*

To make a star:

1. Cut a paper pattern for a five-point star using an illustration as reference, or draw one freehand. Using the paper pattern, cut out two pieces of fabric, adding a small seam allowance all round.

2. Right sides together, sew round star leaving one small length unsewn.

3. Trim excess fabric off point seam allowances then turn the star right way out. (You may need a knitting needle to help push star points out.)

4. Stuff the shape with wadding to give a plump shape.

5. Close the small gap by hand sewing.

6. Sew on small sequins and spangles as decorations and attach a loop of cord from one star point to use as a hook.

HOLLY LEAF RUG

Appliquéd motifs are a simple means of decorating for Christmas and they can be sewn on to all kinds of objects such as cushions, duvet covers or quilts. These red felt holly-leaf shapes are attached to a rug by small green wooden buttons and are inspired by the small fabric washers that sit under buttons on bed mattresses. Here they offer additional decoration, but on a quilt or a padded piece of fabric they could be used to hold the top and bottom layers together, fastening the padding in place. We used an inexpensive wool travel rug, perfect for tucking round knees and legs to keep you warm on cold days. If you do not want to reserve the rug for festive occasions only, you can remove the motifs once Christmas is over.

MATERIALS

A tartan wool travel rug ❧ red felt ❧ green buttons ❧ sewing thread

1. Decide on the size and shape of holly leaf you want and draw an outline of it on paper. Work out exactly where you will sew on the leaves to find out how many to make; we decided to attach a leaf at the intersection of one set of white lines on the tartan.

2. Cut out the felt leaves using the paper template.

3. Sew each leaf in to its correct position on the rug using a button to hold the leaf in position. The leaf should be free from the fabric apart from where it is caught under the button.

PAPIER MÂCHÉ BOWLS

We decorated these bowls with gilded leaves and scraps of ribbon and painted over the finished surface with gold paint. Try different papers for special effects. We used some semi-transparent fibrous papers which allow leaves etc. to show through. You can varnish the finished bowls or leave them plain.

MATERIALS

China or glass bowls as moulds ❧ plain white tissue or transparent paper ❧ recycled paper ❧ wallpaper glue ❧ wide paintbrush ❧ gold paint ❧ masking tape ❧ scraps of gold ribbon ❧ gold-painted leaves ❧ petroleum jelly

1. Begin by choosing bowls to use as moulds. Cover the outside surfaces with petroleum jelly to prevent the papier mâché from sticking to them.

2. Mix up a quantity of wallpaper glue and tear or cut the paper into small strips.

3. Begin to paste strips of paper over the outside of the bowl. Remember that the first layer becomes the inside of your finished bowl. Either paste glue onto each strip or paste glue onto the surface and add the paper.

4. Continue until you have built up your required thickness of paper. Paste on any decorative elements just before you apply the last layer of white tissue or transparent paper. Leave to dry slowly in a warm place. This may take several days depending on how thick the paper is.

5. To make a gold-striped bowl, apply strips of masking tape to the bowl and paint between them. Remove the tape when the paint is dry.

FABRIC & YARN BALLS

Here are several different ideas in one for making decorative balls to hang on the tree or to fill a large, shallow bowl. Shades of blue are not in the least traditional but make a welcome change from red or green. The small touches of gold make sure they look festive. Search haberdashery and soft furnishing departments for all kinds of decorative studs or gimp pins to add detail.

MATERIALS

Knitting yarn, such as chenille or silk ❧ cotton wadding or Polystyrene balls (available from craft and model shops) ❧ gold cords of different thicknesses ❧ pins ❧ organdy fabric ❧ gold paint ❧ ribbon ❧ gimp pins ❧ dried flower petals ❧ glue

1. YARN BALL: Wind a length of yarn around the ball base until it is completely covered. You need to keep turning the ball to be sure the yarn is evenly spaced out all over the surface. Secure the end with a pin, or tuck it under another strand of yarn. Add a ribbon band and decorative gimp pin if you wish. Alternatively wind some gold cord over the yarn, followed by some blue yarn, allowing plenty of the gold to show through from underneath.

2. FABRIC STRIP BALL: Cut bias strips of fabric and wrap these around the ball base until it is completely covered. Pin end in place or use a gimp pin or stud.

3. ORGANDY BALL: Paint a ball with gold paint, leave it to dry, then wrap it in a square of fabric and pull the edges together. Fasten with cord or ribbon.

4. FLOWER PETAL BALL: Glue dried flower petals at regular intervals over the whole surface of the ball. Decorate with ribbon or cord.

BEESWAX CANDLES IN GLASSES

Here we used sturdy clear glass tumblers with a slightly tapering shape. You will need to find proper candle wicks which must be the correct diameter for the size of candle you are making. (You can check this when you buy the wick as its packet should include information about sizing.)

MATERIALS

White candle wax granules ❧ *beeswax (use about one quarter beeswax to three quarters wax granules)* ❧ *wick to fit* ❧ *strong glass tumblers* ❧ *candle putty or Plasticine* ❧ *wooden sticks or skewers* ❧ *double saucepan*

1. Cut wick to depth of glass plus 5cm (2in) extra. Hold wick in place in the middle of the bottom of the glass using a small piece of candle putty or Plasticine.

2. Place stick across top of glass and hold in place with Plasticine at either side. Hang wick over this stick in centre of glass. Fix wick to stick with Plasticine.

3. In a double saucepan melt wax granules and beeswax together until dissolved. Take care if using a gas hob as wax burns easily. Pour the melted wax gently to avoid splashing into the glass, leaving a small space at the top of about 3cm (1in).

4. When set, trim wick leaving about 2cm (¾in) protruding.

ADVENT CALENDAR

An envelope to open for every day in December makes for a completely different kind of Advent calendar. You don't have to fill each one with gifts or sweets. Instead, try putting a joke in each envelope, or a puzzle, or a cryptic clue leading up to something special on the last day. If you doubt your drawing and writing skills, cut out numbers and letters from newspapers or magazines. Once the envelope has been opened for a certain day, unpeg it from the board to show where you are up to.

MATERIALS

One or two large sheets of card (ours is corrugated) ❧ *24 small brown envelopes* ❧ *24 wooden clothes pegs* ❧ *gold paint* ❧ *pencils, paint* ❧ *glue* ❧ *cord, string* ❧ *stars, scraps, felt etc.*

1. Lay out the envelopes in a sequence to fit the card. Two rows of twelve, three rows of eight, or whatever you prefer. Mark where to glue the pegs.

2. Paint wooden pegs with gold paint and leave to dry, then glue in place.

3. Number each envelope as creatively as you can.

4. Put the gifts, sweets or jokes of your choice in each envelope and clip them into pegs.

5. Hang the board from bulldog clips or attach a cord across the back.

RIBBON & GLASS CRYSTAL DROPS

It is possible to buy odd glass drops from old chandeliers in antique and junk shops. They make very special decorations to attach to the tree or, as here, wired to glass candlesticks. You can decorate the ribbons with tiny glass pearls and beads. If you cut off the ribbons somewhere along the length of the glass drop then the beads on the ends touch the glass and make a lovely tinkling sound. You can vary the ribbons so that some are tied in a bow and some just looped in half.

MATERIALS

An assortment of glass chandelier drops ❧ *ribbon* ❧ *tiny glass and pearl beads* ❧ *sewing thread* ❧ *needle* ❧ *scissors* ❧ *pliers* ❧ *fine wire*

1. Decide whether to make a bow or to leave the ribbon plain. Gauge roughly the length of ribbon you will need, according to the size of the drops and whether or not you want a bow.

2. Sew back of bow to wire which runs through the centre of the top of the drop. If there isn't one, make a wire loop with small pliers.

3. For a plain ribbon without a bow, sew a few stitches through the centre of the ribbon and gather it up. Sew it firmly in place at the top of the wire where it is attached to the glass drop.

4. If you tie the ribbon into a bow, decorate the ends of the bows by sewing on small beads. Add more beads at the top, where the ribbon joins the glass drop, or wherever else you choose.

5. Make a loop from fine wire and twist it round top of drop to attach.

CHRISTMAS STOCKING

In most households the tradition of hanging up a stocking is one of the highlights of the festive season. Ready-made stockings are never quite big enough or the right shape. By making your own you can choose the size you want and have fun decorating it. Upholsterer's hessian makes an excellent fabric.

MATERIALS

A piece of hessian, 90x80cm (36x32in) ❧ *sewing thread* ❧ *raffia in four colours* ❧ *embroidery thread in two or more colours* ❧ *scissors* ❧ *paper for template*

1. Cut a paper template then cut two stocking shapes from the hessian. Sew together, ideally making French seams to avoid fraying edges.

2. Fold top edge back down to make a cuff and make a 6cm (2½in) fringe by pulling threads.

3. To make tassels, cut a bundle of 16cm (6½in) lengths of raffia and tie together in middle. Fold bundle in half, then tie round top, about 1.5cm (¾in) down. Attach tassels to cuff and toe of stocking.

4. Make whorls of raffia or embroidery thread by first tying plaits of three strands of thread or raffia. Tie these at top and bottom then coil them to make flat discs. Sew small stitches to hold the coils in place.

5. Use lengths of plaited thread to attach coils to stocking or sew coils flat onto fabric.

CHRISTMAS CRACKER

This larger cracker is meant as a splendid gift wrapping. Don't expect to be able to pull it; making real crackers involves specialist materials.

MATERIALS

Thin card ❧ recycled paper ❧ gold paper ribbon ❧ paper rosette (doiley) ❧ gold fabric ribbon ❧ unbleached paper curling ribbon ❧ gold stars ❧ paper lace ribbon ❧ gilded leaves ❧ glue ❧ double-sided tape ❧ thin string or cord

1. Make a tube from a piece of thin card to the size of the central section of the cracker. Make two smaller tubes to make the sections at each end.

2. Cut paper for body of cracker slightly longer than the three tubes together, including a space between tubes of about 1.5cm (⅝in). Lay the three tubes side by side on the inside of the flat paper, leaving the spaces (see above) between them and stick them to the paper with double-sided tape.

3. Tuck gifts inside central tube then roll the outer paper round the tubes and glue, or stick with double-sided tape.

4. Wrap a small piece of string around the gap between tubes and very gently pull it tight, lapping one end over the other. This takes a little patience and care, but suddenly the paper will give and pull inwards. Tie string tightly and snip off excess. Now decorate with strips of paper ribbon and a paper rosette in the centre; stick on stars and gold leaves.

GENERAL INFORMATION &
EQUIPMENT

WIRE

Wire comes in a vast range of thicknesses, colours and materials, most of which are available from florist's suppliers. Throughout the book two basic kinds of wire are required.

FINE WIRE Where fine wire is specified, you can use the thin wire sold on a reel and known as reel or mossing wire. Rose wire is an even finer wire, sold on a reel or in ready-cut lengths.

MEDIUM WIRE Where medium-thickness wire is required, use the slightly thicker wire sold on a reel or stub wire, which is sold in ready-cut lengths, usually by weight, and comes in various thicknesses. A medium thickness will bend easily but still stay upright when necessary. If you are buying it in lengths, the 25cm (10in) length is the most useful.

Always cut wire with special wire cutters and don't be tempted to use ordinary scissors or your best secateurs.

GLUE GUN

Throughout the book I used an electric glue gun, which is very quick and easy to use when there is a lot of gluing to be done. It is not advisable to use a glue gun for small-scale or fiddly work, however, as the glue may show on the finished piece. Remember to work quickly with a glue gun as the glue cools down fast and is then no longer malleable.

OTHER TOOLS

The most useful equipment to have to hand for the projects in this book are: a straight edge or rule, preferably made from metal, for measuring and cutting against; sharp scissors for cutting fabric; a craft knife or sharp scissors for cutting papers; secateurs for cutting twigs and foliage.

Most projects take up very little space, but a flat surface which will not be harmed by the odd splash of paint or cut from a knife is essential for working on. Take anything to be sprayed with paint outdoors or rig up a background screen to protect whatever is around the object.

INDEX

Advent calendar, 85
amaryllis and leaves, 49
apple and orange garlands, 16

berries, strings, 20–2
bowls, papier mâché, 76
brocade treasure bags, 58

candles: beeswax, 80
    oyster-shell, 60
chandelier, twig, 41
Christmas tree shapes, 70
citrus fruits, carved, 10
cracker, 92

dough shapes, 66

fabric and yarn balls, 79
flowers: dried flower and
    leaf garland, 46
    green and white, 27
    scented posy, 34
fruit: frosted, 30
    fruit basket, 36
    strings, 20–2

garlands, 16, 46
glass, painted, 65
glue guns, 94

heart wreath, 12
holly leaf rug, 72
hyacinth bowl, 42

kissing bough, 33

leaves: dried flower and leaf
        garland, 46
    leaf table decoration, 53
    strings, 20–2
lichen tree, 15

marzipan pears, 44

nuts, strings, 20–2

oak leaf wreath, gilded, 24
oyster-shell candles, 60

paperchains, 62
papier mâché bowls, 76
pears, marzipan, 44
posy, scented, 34

ribbon and glass crystal
        drops, 86
rug, holly leaf, 72

salt dough shapes, 66

scented posy, 34
silver twig bundle, 50
spice, berry and petal balls, 28
stocking, Christmas, 88

table decoration, leaf, 53
treasure bags, brocade, 58
trees: tall moss tree and star, 54
    tall tree with marzipan pears;
        44
twigs: silver twig bundle, 50
    twig chandelier, 41
    twig-wrapped gilded globes,
        18

wire, 94
wreaths, 12, 24

ACKNOWLEDGMENT
The publishers would like to
thank Jayne Keeley of Country
Living Magazine for permission
to reproduce the following projects devised by her: Heart
Wreath (p.12), Fruit Basket
(p.36). The Brocade Treasure
Bags (p.58) were also based on
an idea by Jayne Keeley.